Published in the UK by
POWERFRESH Limited
3 Gray Street
Northampton
NN1 3QQ

Telephone 01604 630 996
Facsimile 01604 621 013
E Mail   pwrfresh@nccnet.co.uk

Copyright © 1998 Paul Whorton Illustrations by Andrew Grunden

Cover and interior layout by Powerfresh

ISBN 1 874125 856

D1460830

Sales

All rights reserved. No part of this publication may be
reproduced or transmitted in any form or by any means,
electronic or mechanical,including photocopying, recording
or any information storage and retrieval system, or for the
source of ideas without the written permission of the publisher.

Printed in the UK by Avalon Print Northampton
Powerfresh September 1998

PROUD to be BALD

THE ESSENTIAL SURVIVOR'S GUIDE

By Paul Whorston

Illustrations by Andrew Grunden

THE PERFECT GIFT

FOR _____

FROM _____

EARLY WARNING SIGNS

... like

huge ears ...

freckles ...

an odd shaped
head ...

unsightly scars ...

.. or

even

worse ...

ALL

of them!!

Just when your

image starts to

fall into place ...

... your
hair starts
to fall
OUT!!

After playing with your favourite rubber duck ...

always be prepared for ...

Useful tip:-

Get your best friend to pull the plug out!

Interesting fact:-

Mature males lose on average between 30 and 100 hairs every day but not usually in one shampoo!

... a hair raising SURPRISE!!

In
romance ...

... first
impressions
count,

unfortunately!!

Real Truth:-

Most women find bald men sexy!

Transport minister Reginald
Smog takes to the bus ...

... happy in the knowledge that public
transport is the safest
and most relaxed way to
travel ...

... oblivious,
Reginald
meets the
day
FACE ON!!

When youthful pleasures no longer inspire ...

... and comforting dreams are all you desire ...

... don't set your head on fire!!

Useful tip:-

When going abroad take a snorkel tube and bury your head in the sand.

THE COMB OVER

(this requires plenty of grease and gel)

The side 'Comb-Over'

The back 'Comb-Over'

The front 'Comb-Over'

With a little imagination, some very decorative effects can be achieved with a combination of 'Comb-Over' techniques ...

... the ULTIMATE 'Comb-Over'!!

Lotions, potions, rubbing motions ...

... not one more hair - it don't seem fair!!

Out of the window with the lot!!

To cultivate the garden plot!!

Healthy hair tip:-

Moisturise your hair and soothe your scalp with
this easy recipe:-

Mix a small pot of yoghurt with one teaspoon of honey and a liquidised quarter of chicken manure, apply to dry hair and leave for 10 minutes if you dare!

WIGS

When choosing a wig you must make sure ...

... it's not too small,

or too big ...

and it suits your life- style!!

Easy Rider ...

with real style?

in a HELMET!!

The future is bright ...

... the future is SHINY!!

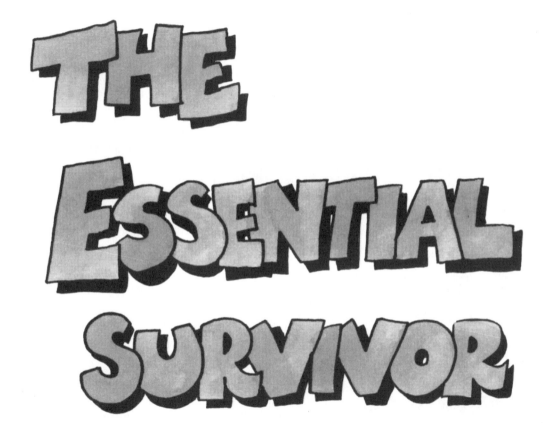

If you are loosing yours
when all about you have still
got theirs ...

then a friend in need ...

is a
friend
in...

DEED!!

Accidents do happen!!

And hurtful abuse will often follow ...

... but sometimes you just
might find, you can get ...

the
last
LAUGH!!

Usual, Sir? ...

... More off the sides, Sir?

The
cleanest
cut of
ALL!!

When all seems lost ...

Do not despair about your hair ...

... use
your
HEAD!!

Bald Qualities

- ❏ Charm
- ❏ Sexy
- ❏ Intelligent
- ❏ Wisdom
- ❏ Leadership
- ❏ Sporty
- ❏ Witty
- ❏ Suave
- ❏ Handsome
- ❏ A one in a million
- ❏ All of them

Tick the box or boxes which most applies to the recipient of this book.

For a Bald & Proud
T-shirt please
telephone or fax
01566 782789
or write to
E.S.G. CREATIONS.

TITLES BY
POWERFRESH
· NORTHAMPTON · ENGLAND ·

CRINKLED 'N' WRINKLED

TRUE LOVE

OH NO IT'S XMAS AGAIN

FUNNY SIDE OF 30s

FUNNY SIDE OF 40 HIM

FUNNY SIDE OF 40 HER

FUNNY SIDE OF 50 HIM

FUNNY SIDE OF 50 HER

FUNNY SIDE OF 60'S

FUNNY SIDE OF SEX

GOLFAHOLICS

MIDLIFE CRISIS

WE'RE GETTING MARRIED

THE DEFINITIVE GUIDE TO VASECTOMY

KEEP FIT WITH YOUR CAT

PMT CRAZED

HORNY MAN'S ADULT DOODLE BOOK

HORNY GIRL'S ADULT DOODLE BOOK

IF BABIES COULD TALK

CAT CRAZY

MAD TO TRAVEL BY AIR...

MAD TO PLAY GOLF...

MAD TO HAVE A BABY...

MAD TO GET MARRIED...

MAD TO HAVE A PONY

THE OFFICE FROM HELL

MAD TO HAVE A CAT

MAD TO HAVE A COMPUTER

YOU DON'T HAVE TO BE MAD TO BE 40 HIM

YOU DON'T HAVE TO BE MAD TO BE 40 HER

YOU DON'T HAVE TO BE MAD TO BE 50 HIM

YOU DON'T HAVE TO BE MAD TO BE 50 HER

MAD ON FOOTBALL

MAD TO BE A MOTHER

MAD TO BE A FATHER

THE BARE BOTTOM BOOK

GOOD WHILE IT LASTED

FUNNY FARM SILLY MOOS

FUNNY FARM PIGGERY JOKERY

PROUD TO BE BALD

DICKS NAUGHTY BOOK

For more information on these or other titles please write to :
Powerfresh Ltd. 3 Gray Street, Northampton, NN1 3QQ, ENGLAND.
Telephone 01604 630 996 Fax 01604 621 013
E Mail pwrfresh@ nccnet.co.uk